My Thoughts on Life's Intimate Wonders

My Thoughts on Life's Intimate *Wonders*

A COLLECTION OF PERSONAL AND SPIRITUAL ESSAYS

VIVIAN ANN VELASCO

XULON PRESS

Xulon Press
2301 Lucien Way #415
Maitland, FL 32751
407.339.4217
www.xulonpress.com

© 2021 by Vivian Ann Velasco

All rights reserved solely by the author. The author guarantees all contents are original and do not infringe upon the legal rights of any other person or work. No part of this book may be reproduced in any form without the permission of the author. The views expressed in this book are not necessarily those of the publisher.

Due to the changing nature of the Internet, if there are any web addresses, links, or URLs included in this manuscript, these may have been altered and may no longer be accessible. The views and opinions shared in this book belong solely to the author and do not necessarily reflect those of the publisher. The publisher, therefore, disclaims responsibility for the views or opinions expressed within the work.

Unless otherwise indicated,Scripture quotations taken from the King James Version (KJV) – *public domain.*

Paperack ISBN-13: 978-1-6628-2958-1
Hardcover ISBN-13: 978-1-6628-3002-0
Ebook SBN-13: 9781--6628-2959-8

Ron Seman, Indiana Dunes Photographer and hiking guide donated his photograph for the cover of my collection. His strong eye of God's beauty at the Dunes is a comfort for us all.

Sunsets are a passion of mine. As I look onto his work, the movement of the bird in flight reminds me to open wings and soar high. As I look on the water at this scared place, I'm reminded of where we all came from and the power that Our Lord has over our lives and day to day presence here on His earth.

This collection is a journey through life with God on my side.

I dedicate this book to my
wonderful family and friends,
with an inside smile.

To my father who
helped me put my first words to paper.
You have all touched me and given me smiles and
the ability to laugh and find myself.
For that I'm very grateful.

Table of Contents

My favorite photos to share with my readers 1
Words. 3
Precious Memories. 5
We Forgot: An Easter Message 7
The Art of Dying. 11
Sisters. 13
The Art of Caring 15
Fighting Our Addictions 19
The Path We All Must Endure. 25
For My Children. 29
Fight Hard 31
Friends. 35
In Love of All God's Creatures 39
Love at First Sight 41
Thanksgiving for Essential Workers 43
Is There a Future for Our Children? 45
My Son 49
My Daughter 53
Dearest Baby 57

A Mother's Eyes..59
My Brother..63
"It's Finished"..65
Our Lord's Work 69
A Runner's Story...71
Joey's Christmas At Sea..73
Afterthoughts upon Completion of My Book 77
Special Thanks...79
About the Author..81

~

My favorite photos to share with my readers

$\mathcal{M}$y entire life I have enjoyed photographs of family, friends and the landscapes around us here on earth. I took these photos throughout the years and have saved them refer back to these sites on many occasions. They give me strength and comfort in good times and bad.

It seemed only fitting that I would share my favorites, giving a promenade location in my collection.

These were taken in northwest Indiana at the Indiana Dunes, where I have experienced comfort, serenity, many laughs, and sometimes tears. Even in the middle of a total rain storm, sitting under a wooden pavilion, I have found beautiful memories and of course laughs at being the only one there during a storm. So, it is a special place for me.

I hope, as my readers, you will see what I see and value the strength and serenity that can surround you from God's fingerprints. I look forward to this Dune's trip every year and hope to continue the tradition for a lifetime.

Words

As a child your mom taught you to use your words softly and with meaning. As we a young adult, we learned early on how words can hurt and cut you to the core. As adults those same words not only hurt but connected with sarcasm or in mockery can change our lives forever. Strange how a word can affect us in our daily routine.

A word can make us smile, bring a tear of joy, sour a day or stay in our minds for the years ahead. They are so powerful and, yet, such a small thing. These words were chosen for you with much consideration. As your friend, we have a bond and a connection. I have listened through the years, and these words suit you and are in my favor.

Choose your words wisely, as they can cut like a knife,
or sooth a broken heart.

It is so sad that poorly selected words and phrases can break up a family for years to come. With all your strength, never let this happen. Family needs the force we get from one another in day-to-day life or in any crisis.

Keep your words in this little pouch in your pocket or purse or anywhere near you. When you are hurt, distressed, or in pain, know that I'm there for you, and I know the right words to whisper to you. In times we are not together, pull out these specially chosen words and read them and keep them in your mind and heart. They will give you strength. The power of the written word is very strong. I, for one, never doubt how hurtful or how wonderful they can be.

May all words give you pleasure not only for yourself but for one another.

"Nothing is impossible, the word itself says, 'I'm possible.'"
—**Audrey Hepburn**
April 21, 2015, Women's Empowerment Conference, Austin, Texas

Precious Memories

*G*od is so masterful, so all knowing. As He created us all that time ago, He was sure to make our minds ready to take on vast amounts of knowledge. In that creative moment, in His all-mighty care, knowing we are human, He made us with the ability to retain precious memories. As children, we collect objects, things we can hold and carry and easily lose. Through experiences, developing relationships and the capacity of love for another person, we become attached to items so tender to our hearts, we can't begin to explain or express the connection.

With the knowledge and strength our Lord has given us, we try to use it to the fullest. Helping a neighbor, our families, animals, and all who are tender. They call it multitasking. I call it God's full outreach, using our minds, hearts and capabilities for His Word in every moment. Being human, we turn our head for one second, and a moment is lost. A possession misplaced and the dearest is out of our sight. The pain is incredible. These trophies of the earth are so valuable to our spirit and mind's eye. The idea sits in our thoughts that our loved one touched this item day after day and still possess our lost one's fingerprints and oils.

When our time comes to pass on from this world, we go back to the earth that our Savior made for us to walk upon. Precious metals of the valuable gold and silver go back as well. As we have lost the touch, I like to believe it has gone back to the Giver of these precious items. So, in all, remember, they are not lost; they are back with your loved one and waiting for you to join someday when God decides it is your time. They will be waiting for you in some glories and peace, and all your pain will be taken away and forgotten. All is not lost, forgotten, or misplaced. In our beautiful minds, the treasure is stronger, more exact and will continue to please you and give you those precious memories. How they linger to flood your soul with unseen angels all around to protect us!

Therefore, fill your heart with joy. Let your soul be full of song, and although you grieve at this time, you will see and feel such grace and glory as you touch those stars and not only feel that precious memory, but it will be returned to you with a touch and spirit we can't fully understand at this time. The song reads: "How great Thou art." Such a statement of truth and one for us to hold on to.

Lord, my friend needs strength. One thing after another has left her breathless and dismayed. Lift her chin, strengthen her faithful stance, and then encourage her to walk again with you. With you all things are possible.
Thank you.

WE FORGOT: AN EASTER MESSAGE

As these months pass us by, we continue to be unaware of God's focus and concern for our lives. We may read the old scriptures and find high storms, burning bushes, and acts of violence. In these modern times, we have believed and come to expect those signs from our Lord don't exist anymore. How wrong could we be? How could we have fallen from such grace that we totally missed the signs. The signs God has left for us are for everlasting peace and purity. I'm sad to look back and see how we missed the mark on so many occasions. God is now speaking in these modern times, expressing himself in ways that we are finding it hard to accept.

This coronavirus plague that has come down to this earth is strong, deadly, and all encompassing. What in the world have we done? What could have been so bad to see the deaths of so many and such intolerance? Our loved ones have all been touched, bullied, and condemned. In the year 2020, who could ever foresee these constant reminders that God is unhappy with us and has probably had the last straw while He watches on in our daily lives.

As I look around and open my eyes, I am reminded that we have forgotten some basic prayers and thoughts that our Lord has laid out before us for so many years, with His presence so many years ago, to the scripture and sermons we look up to now in the present. We forgot. We became too earthly involved; too many material objects have clouded our way. The storms hit us, and we try to buy it away with earthly monies, wealth, and thoughts of evil pleasures here on earth. We forgot. We put all those wonderful stories of our God in the back of our minds, or we disassociated from them all together.

At this time of Easter, we are humbled and brought back to the importance things of our lives. The messages left before are for us to read for generations to come. Whether you believe or not, there is something there— place of peace we all long for, a touch on a shoulder, and the smile of another. It all comes from the same place in our hearts. As I stay enclosed in my home following the rules of today, fighting this plague, this evil that has come before all this earth, I see and feel the simple things of life, this beautiful bounty all around us. A touching phone call that at one time I wouldn't have time to answer. Simple gestures from a neighbor standing from a distance, a smile for a shut in, a simple wave, I know we can make it, and I'm reminded that we forgot the importance of the simple things. They may not cost a dime, can't be purchased or delivered online, and are valued so much more than words can express.

We may or may not be given a second chance to get this right. Wars need to end, such hatred feelings and talk needs to end for another person. Aren't we all the same? Human beings walking on this earth trying to create a world for ourselves that God has meant for us to have. Sadness and criticism need to disintegrate. Our words hurt so desperately. Can we get that kindness back? Can we get the simpler ways of life back on track? I don't know. It is a mystery.

After losses and sadness in my life, I did forget. I forgot to ask for help to lead the way. Through the last months, signs have been in front of me: a cancer struggle, hurtful days for my son, the loss of family and friends, I'm surprised to say I have opened my eyes to the importance of life and how we spread the Word. God won't do things to harm us, but He will show His unhappiness in unique ways to show us the way and lead us back to the values of life. It may be by hearing a soft sermon from a beloved pastor or understanding the words and putting them first in our lives. Offering a hand to one who is hurting, or an unexpected flower giving that person hope and a smile for better times ahead is one way to share His love.

We all forgot. It is now our time to show we get it. We understand how we need to get back to basics, valuing our lives and the spoken words of others. We need to be using our listening ears and less our mouths, continuing to create more memories for generations to come.

For all who have given me kindness in these hard times, I express myself through my words of appreciation and love for all of you. Our Lord has given me that talent and touches my soul with strength and comfort to help others. May this Easter bring some peace to you and your family, and guide you to make better decisions of comforting another with the art of listening. We forgot, but we are forgiven for that lack of judgment, and we have been given another chance. May this season in our trials of today here on earth bring your strength and a zeal to help others open their hearts to all of mankind.

"Then He arose and rebuked the wind, and said to the sea, "peace, be still!" And the wind ceased and there was a great calm."
—**Mark 4:39**

"Be strong and courageous. Do not be afraid or terrified because of them, for the Lord your God goes with you: He will never leave you nor forsake you."
—**Deuteronomy 31:6**

The Art of Dying

None of us are promised one moment on this earth. Hearing this expression for so many years as I've grown older, I've pondered that thought of late. Through the years, we lose loved ones without notice. We can be shocked over the loss of neighbors, friends, and family, not understanding why their precious lives were taken from us. As a God-fearing woman, I have come to realize in my mature years that no matter the age or the circumstances, God has plans for us all. His timeline is not ours and never will be. I've had many losses in my life and have often wondered why they were meant to go so young, or of so much talent, or with so much to offer, and I've never received an answer, until now. I don't believe in predestination in our lifetimes because I believe that God gave us strong minds, strong wills, and the ability to make choices. He will guide us, teach us the way, and lead us in the right direction, but it is up to us as human beings to make those decisions and values for our lives here on earth.

"I will instruct you and teach you in the way which you should go:
I will counsel you with My eye upon you."
—Psalm 32:8

We forget at times that we are of God's creation, subject to His masterful plan, as we inhabit this earth. Rather than grieve over our own personal losses, I believe we need to remember that the Lord takes us for what lays before us so perfectly in heaven where there is no more pain, no more grief of earthly problems, and such beauty we can't begin to imagine.

In our hearts we know that being taken to be with the Lord is a step to grace. Being able to sit at His side, and being reunited and see others of our past are a joy we have been living and dreaming for. I've always hoped to find our precious animals we loved for so many years at that time. God has that plan, and we need to accept and have faith in His decisions to take us, no matter when and fulfill duties far above us. After losing two infants on this earth so many years ago, I like to believe that God has them in his arms as angels helping all of us below. They had a purpose by His side as well as so many others around us that have gone way too early. Young or old, we are taken for reasons only God can justify.

I pray for all that are waiting to see His shining face, touch his robes, and hear the gentle tone of His voice. Don't be afraid; don't be scared. All of life's secrets will be answered and your peace all encompassing. Don't give us a moment of thought as we are left behind. We will join you when our time comes and see those treasures in your company. We will follow your example and know your pain is gone and all beauty before all of us.

"The Lord is my shepherd; I shall not want. He makes me lie down in green pastures; He leads me beside the still waters. He restores my soul: He leads me in the paths of righteousness for His name's sake. Yea, though I walk through the valley of the shadow of death, I will fear no evil: for You are with me: your rod and Your staff, they comfort me.
—Psalm 23:1–4

Sisters

Reaching out to touch a tender cheek, a strong hand and an extended arm that is meant for hugging on a nothing day, the tender sound of a gentle voice or whisper, the connected mind and overlapping thoughts, all come to mind of sisters around the world. The grace of God can be seen in your faces, sometimes a familiar look, or an identical look. One thing is for sure, sisters are fortunate enough to share a bond and connection that can only come from our Lord. Your association was planned so long ago as God has commanded. In His eyes, your favor is shown in one another. Your individual uniqueness shines through in every breath, every smile, and every tear. You both may pattern one another, but you both possess qualities that are all together rare. How God must love all sisters so dearly since He saw fit to duplicate many features in each of you, passed down from friend to friend. Yes, indeed friends—the strongest of bonds, the genuine language, and loud silences between both of you. Such a magical thought that your presence will be felt in each other and families for generations to come.

As the years go on, the storms of life can become fierce and strong. A division has occurred and so foreign in your mind that you would never believe that the person so connected to you has turned their back and forgotten all the strength and compassion you have for one another. Sadly, days and years can go by with not a word spoken. Never let this happen in your lifetime. Don't be afraid to get past the storm and cling to one another as your hearts bond back together again. Words are powerful and strong. They can cut like a knife or sooth a broken heart. God gives you the power to hold on to each other tight and get past any winding road that sisters may come against.

There are no stumbles, no twisted paths, that can not be overcome. The winds may pick up speed and throw you to the ground, but with our Lord's hand, sisters are intertwined and can overcome any hurtle together. As Christ gives us the strength to continue through the longest of journeys, the tallest of mountains, sisters will always feel the pain of one another and fight with all the fight within them to get through any pain—together.

Please heed these words and meaning behind these words from the book of John:

"Anyone who loves their brother and sister lives in the light, and there is nothing in them to make them stumble."
—1 John 2:10

The Art of Caring

Within ourselves we need to look deep into our hearts. We have answers deep inside. You need the strength to give and survive every day. Look to yourself to see the truth. The truth is, you are a caregiver who never gives in no matter how tired you are, and you continue searching the roads ahead. You are in the company of someone that is alone, weak, and may have lost their way. The passion you feel within yourself is deep, and you give to others every day of your life. The hope you have for others is immeasurable. Your strength carries on, no matter how tired you are, and you give others hope and the benefits of your love. Your compassion is strong and will calm any storm. You pass on your strength day in and day out. It is part of you and your being. God has nurtured you for that reason. You never give up and never run away from giving of yourself and your time to others.

The people you are comforting every day look forward to your welcoming smile, strong arms, and soft eyes. You may be the only person they see in a day, and leaving part of yourself with them is a gracious gift. Their journey and path of many tall mountains is very hard and causes the loss of confidence and loss of passion for life. You tame these mountains are tamed and show your strength in guiding to the other side. It is a struggle for such lonely people, but with the first words from your lips, you help climb those mountains and keep each person pushing on.

May God give you the strength and wisdom to continue helping others in need. Never forget you are much appreciated, even though it may be unspoken. You leave your mark every day with compassion and desire to help others.

*"The Lord gives strength to his people;
the Lord blesses his people with peace."*
—Psalm 29:11

Fighting Our Addictions

*"For I know the plans I have for you," declares the Lord,
"plans to prosper you and not to harm you,
plans to give you hope and a future."*
—*Jeremiah 29:11*

The hole goes on and on, never ending. Your fingernails are full of black dirt from scratching the curved walls. Your hair smells of sweat and foul never realized before. The caked mud on your arms, legs, and neck itch and remind you of your own filth. Continuing down the this dark, damp, and gloomy passageway, I dream of better times. It haunts me day in and day out as if this is my torment in life, to search my mind and see the good things in my world, such as a loving family, beautiful children, and a bounty of the bright sun against my face. What happened? I know falling from grace in such a way that the earth is swallowing you up with no way out. There is no more sun, no touch of a child against my face, no sweetness in life.

None of this torment came overnight. I ignored and put aside so many days, never appreciating what I had, what God gave for the respect of this earth. I'm now a part of the bad things of hell. The flames grow louder, the continuous hurts, and ongoing tortures of life have attacked me in such a way that I can never get out. This all becomes a cycle. See the light, a way out, a future; then it goes away and too far out of your reach only to go back into that hole again. The dripping of hot water on my face from this horrible place is attacking my brain. I can't breathe anymore, can't go forward and can't go back.

The influences of life invaded me, and as I lay alone in these surrounding, I understood. I had taken the sweetness of Jesus and threw all aside. I made a mockery of the wonderful bounty surrounding me on this beautiful earth. I forgot all His words and allowed an ugliness to enter my body, never fighting, never standing up to the lusts of life. My body isn't mine anymore. It is just a shell of what could have been. As I think about this world and what I gave up for the taste of evil, I'm saddened and ashamed.

Suddenly, I feel a strength I've not felt before—a light at the end of this place, helping guide me out into the sunlight. Sore muscles work as never before to reach that goal. Crawling and digging, I cry with the thoughts of another chance, another twenty-four hours of freedom. I can do this. God, give me the strength to survive and strengthen my mind. Words are starting to come to mind that I must have heard in my former life: "Fear can hold you prisoner; hope can set you free." As I keep saying it, feeling it, the light begins to get stronger and steadier in my head. I feel the fresh air, the sweetness it has to offer. Fear, loss, and lack of trust in my Lord got me here to this place, and with His words and counseling, I think I can make it out. Coming closer and closer, please don't close the door—please keep the doorway open. What a horrible thought to have the entranceway close on me as I get closer, a real sign of hell. Please, let me out, let me see the light, let me feel the wind through my soiled hair.

Making it through that doorway, I see it all, feel it all with such a grace I've never felt before. On my knees, I pray to God to help me continue to a new life. Working hard to fight this torment and lust I feel now, I can see the brightness the world has to offer without mockery. My brain has forever been changed and is ready for all that God has to offer. Addiction to the horrors of life can break you in all ways. With God's help and the touch of family and friends, guidance is before you if you can just reach out and touch it. It is there for the taking. May the horrors of addiction never touch your soul again. You have been given another path, not an easy one, but one that the Lord will help you cross each day. Let His arms swallow you every moment of every day when the pain becomes strong. The rough waters ahead will be a challenge and at times unforgivable. Just remember His touch, the wonders of His eyes watching over you, then receive that comfort you need to face each day.

Let tears and that anguish fly away from the heaviness of your body. Open your arms and soar. Glide way high above the mountains. It is never easy, not meant to be. Fight as you never have before to keep the wonders of life that our Lord has given us. Never forget this experience, your second chance. Keep pushing because stumbles are a daily fight. Every day will be an open sore ready to fester. Don't let it. Keep fighting and with God's tremendous love, you will make it and be loved on the other side.

With His hand on your back, work hard to climb with all the strength you have within you. Feel the courage, the compassion, and all the love our Lord can give you. Let loose and feel it. It may knock you down every day for the rest of your life. Be strong and get back up; push on, and dust yourself off. Always going to be challenge, a sadness that evil will use to pull you back in, stand strong and move those mountains to see the wonders that life can bring.

Have control of your life. Let courage be your path and realize how much you are loved on this earth and in heaven. Yes, you lost your way for a second; the timeline of your life, like sands on a beach, is just a concept and shows us how small we are in this life. Be strong and raise yourself up and fight hard. Life is good, and your ability to help others with this fight is tremendous. Trust in our Lord and in yourself. He will never steer you in the wrong direction.

"Recovery didn't open the Gates of Heaven and let me in, Recovery opened the Gates of Hell and let me out."
—**Anonymous**

The Path We All Must Endure

As time goes on, as people of this world, we learn that we are not promised one day, one minute, or one second. God keeps a careful watch over our steps and direction in this lifetime. This is a curiosity to me and one I have pondered over for some time now. Our paths, guided throughout life, live deep within us. As children of God, we must work hard to pull out these thoughts and develop them. This is a gift and not to be to be taken lightly. The glitches in the road, the bumps on our paths, don't sink our lives. They inspire our lives.

I was given the opportunity to meet a young man far beyond his years, with strength coming from and developed by his entire family. Joshua was born into this mother's arms, so that with all the strength and wonder in his eyes, the Lord saw a different path for this little person in His mind's eye. After thirteen days, the light of his mother's heart, was challenged; put on trial, and the need for strength was upon a hurting family. With the love of God and family, Joshua has continued throughout his life with challenges but, never more than he could handle. As we have been told many times, the Lord does not give us more than we can handle. Joshua's closely beloved family took those words and planted them deep within their hearts and minds.

We must remember that people in our lives, along the way of the many years, leave a footprint on our souls. Seldom recognized or felt, these prints mold our lives throughout our years. We can use that strength or pass it along as if it never existed. Using this knowledge is silver and gold, never tarnished, never broken. Josh came into my life when I was teaching high school, and I immediately saw a touching side of him, with his wonderful sense of humor, all-around honesty, and zest for life, I knew immediately we would become friends and that our paths had crossed for a higher reason. Not long after our meeting in the classroom, I had the opportunity to meet his mother. All my questions and thoughts about his personality were solved. Jill is an outstanding woman and leader. She has all the strength I knew she would possess. Josh was diagnosed at the early age of thirteen days, with cerebral palsy, but I could see passion in his mother's eyes that turned this tragedy, as some would say, into the purest joy of a human being, her son.

As our paths continued to grow wider throughout the school year, our lives were put to the test. Coming from a huge support system called a family, many obstacles and back steps were to take place, not only in Josh's family, but my own. Never did I see this young man waver or give up his strength to continue that path that the Lord laid out for us. From his overwhelming desire to put one step in front of the other, I became so enthralled with the presence of our God and the road I was traveling, I became more aware of this wonderful world around us, the bounty our Lord has laid out for us and wanting us to see.

Journeys have a way of throwing us for a curve, a hairpin curve. As much as we remember, these curves and paths are directed by God, they nonetheless test our strength and power over ourselves. In my own personal journey, I became aware of my weaknesses. Cancer had invaded my body with no notice or appointment. Devastated and beat down from this update on my life, I turned my weakness to my friend. Without a second, Josh began to lay out God's plan and path for my life. I began to realize God has a bigger plan for me, a bigger knowledge of the world.

Through this process I have felt and observed divine connections. Those connections bounced me off to what I thought was a straight path to a path of unusual relationships, opportunities, and life experiences I needed for the future. I believe this is how I met Josh. His work ethic, sincerity, and kindness of thoughts with profound strength gave me the fight in my soul to work and cut out this disease from my body. With the connection of doctors, hospitals, treatments, and my friend, a heavy load has been tamed and lifted.

Our paths continue to cross and remain interconnected and close. Josh and his outstanding love of life, family, and God has encouraged me to continue along the heavy path of beating cancer. As a young man who fought for the strength to walk, climb stairs, speak with that wonderful voice of his, Josh's pathway to the future is very bright. From his perspective, and all those who know him, the dreaded diagnosis of cerebral palsy and a life of living in a wheel chair have been tossed out the window. With work, determination, a zeal for life, and a loving family, this young man surpasses all the odds every day of his life. The wheelchair is no more, the walker stands at attention only for times of tired muscles, and the cane has become his livelihood. From the statement very early on that Josh would never walk or talk, he is a miracle in the making, a witness that our God's hand is on our shoulders every step of the path, every step of the journey.

My journey is no longer bleak. My eyes have been opened, and I see life through Joshua and all he has accomplished. It isn't over. Life is ahead of us all. Take the time and your belief, no matter how modest, and shelter—strongly guard—the thoughts your belief sparks for the illumination of the bright days ahead. Know we are all given the strength to carry on even if we think we have no strength left. It is a gift and one I treasure.

"Strength and courage do not come from winning. Your struggles develop, your strengths. When you go through hardships and decide not to surrender, that is strength."
—**Arnold Schwarzenegger**

For My Children

A daily prayer for you, from me.

Never forget that I love you.
Life is filled with hard times and good times.
Learn from everything and everyone you can.
Be the man and woman I know you can be.
I'll think of you every day as you fight for your life to come back to you.
I'm only a moment away.

"Only guard yourself and guard your soul carefully, lest you forget the things your eyes saw, and lest these things depart your heart all the days of your life. And you shall make them known to your children, and to your children's children."
—**Holocaust Museum**

Fight Hard

Cancer is such a foreign word. An ugly word and one that we hope we can be fortunate enough to avoid in our lifetimes. As we walk these hard roads of life, at times it is impossible for us to run away. In our minds, we know that God has a forever plan for us, but it is hard to understand the whys of such crises in our lives. You have hit this mountain hard with a lot of rocks and debris in the way of a lifetime walk. You have to wonder, *Why me*? In all types of situations, we ask ourselves these questions and continuously contemplate the whys of such hard fortune. I know the questions in your mind. You see them so clearly. We see through the tears and long to be held and comforted by our loved ones to tell us this isn't happening, but indeed it is.

Life throws us these curves, least expected and most dreaded, but somehow, we stand tall and remember we are not in it alone. We are not alone and separated from friends, family, and most of all, our Lord. As we looked out our windows this winter and spring, we see God's great bounty before us, reminding us every day that He encircles us every day. When we look upon a child and into their eyes, they know the passion of our Lord and spread it to us with each look, glance, and word spoken—words of hope and unconditional love that only a child can share with us. A hand on your cheek, a hug with those small arms give us the world to cling to.

This is a long journey for all of us, with stumbles along the way. We must embrace God's love, direction, and kindness to us. In every little obstacle, every fall in this path, we know He is there for us, guiding us to the next step, no matter how hard. When the sun breaks through these gloomy days, we can feel on our faces His strength, and passion for our wellbeing. Enjoy these days and be comforted that you are not alone at all.

We all have strengths for help us in this world. Yours is compassion for others, and in all your pain and weakness in illness, you go on and continue to help others and support others. Never let this special personality get past you. It is a gift from God. We all have those wonderful gifts and need to treasure them. Christ always has interesting plans for us. To my surprise, mine was getting cancer. I know that sounds odd, but from these divine connections I have made in this fight, I have met wonderful people, and talked and spread the word of His teachings with others. So as my life continues I will forever volunteer and meet people needing help and compassion in this fight of many types of cancers. It is a plan I'll forever cherish from our Lord. My path is clear now, and I hope yours becomes clear as well. Use your strengths to follow this lifelong plan of God's as it touches you and your family.

As the cancer leaves our bodies and becomes a thing of the past, we can feel comfort that we are watched and embraced by people of this earth. You have been chosen for greatness by our Lord, and He will not leave your side or keep you in the dark shadows. There is that wonderful glow and brightness from our beliefs and faith. It won't let you down. Prayers for your continued recovery and wellness as it comes to you.

Fight Hard

"The Lord replied. 'My Presence will go with you, and I will give you rest.'"
—Exodus 33:14

You don't have to be afraid you have the strength and you can push your fears aside. It's a long road. You can find the way and search within yourself. The pain will disappear. You can survive and trust the faith inside yourself. Don't let anyone take this away from you. There will be tomorrows. I promise.

Friends

"For I know the plans I have for you," declares the Lord,
"plans to prosper you and not to harm you,
plans to give you hope and a future."
—Jeremiah 29:11

I love this passage; it gives me power in times of everlasting storms. The reason I hold on is for the continuous ability to rely on another's compassion for life and guidance to achieve my goals. God always has a plan and is forever pushing on. Of course, He gives us strength, but so often here on earth, we need that touch, someone's arms wrapped around us that keep us moving forward with His gentle guidance. We will never understand or be given the knowledge of why we create a bond, a connection, with another. It could be look, a glance, a smile, or hearty giggle that lets us know this person is meant to look inside and know the truth within. Sometimes more clearly than we know ourselves. You can find this love for another deep inside yourself. It may only happen once in a lifetime. God never gives us a number of these acquaintances that may come our way, those divine connections only He can guide, so treasure what you have and find the gift in that fellow person that God has put on your path.

In your eyes, this person may be a hero. Reaching within yourself, you know they are meant for you. God sent them and touched you, and so hope is always in your pocket for the both of you. It's a truth only you can come to realize. Facing the world alone can be cruel. Our Lord never meant for it to be easy by any means. It is with the strength from one another that you know you can survive and face any storm. You see the truth that only you two can share. Don't let anyone take it away. Don't let anyone crush your dreams you have in common. By sharing with one another, you are sharing with our Lord.

Follow your heart and know your friend was placed on earth under our heavenly Father's guidance to carry on and follow those dreams and accomplish anything on your journey. Nothing is impossible, knowing your friend is on your side and in your thoughts. You may come to doubt yourself when outsiders show a side of envy at what you have. It is a sadness for them because they can't begin to understand what you have that has been given to you in this life. They strive for that connection with someone, but it never comes, and they may search for a long time and never feel or understand that relationship. You were chosen to feel this connection. Never debate it or have someone try to take it away with sour words or desires. You will find a way to continue and see and feel the power you have through your friend that leads you ultimately to our Father.

Your friendship means the world to me, and I know how precious it is in my heart. The feelings guide me through each day, and from your strength I receive mine. I am forever grateful.

*"In his heart a man plans his course,
but the Lord determines his steps."*
—Proverbs 16:9

In Love of All God's Creatures

The skies are clear, and the clouds speak to us in all languages of the world. When we follow these paths from our Lord, we are never more aware of the bright spirit and pleasure the landscape around us can bring. As we walk through the vast lands that God has laid out before us, we are at times blessed with the connection of so many creatures around us. That connection is powerful and draws us as human beings to the special impact that an animal can serve in our lives. Never forget, they are a gift from the Lord and need to be sheltered and stroked for unconditional love to be returned in our personal lives. Not all God's creatures have this ability to impact us in such ways. As children of God, we are lucky to have the opportunity, for a short time in this life, to call an animal our friend.

These beasts from God's hands need to be nurtured for the short time we have them in our lives. They give us such pleasure and open our eyes to the world around us. This world is one of peace, beauty, and brightness.

_____, you have given God much pleasure in the care of such a wonderful creature named, _____ and will forever shine in your heart and can be seen in your eyes every day for the rest of your life. It is a compliment to you that God chose you to take care *of this wonderful creature in God's nation. Protect that strength that _____ gave you and know you can put it in the back of your mind, but it will never be far away from your heart.*

Love at First Sight

A sparkle in an eye, a tip of a head to the side, a soothing chuckle, or bright smile—who knows what "love at first sight" really means. I do know it starts off spontaneously but takes years to grow and must be nurtured. As paths cross through the years, the deeper the thoughts become a sting much broader in your memories. Many will look on with jealousy and wonder what the connection may be and gossip about the depth of this relationship, but it is for these two alone. As the years pass, the laugher comes easier. Although soothing, it becomes crisper and with a depth that no one else would understand, much like a private joke between the two. The intimacy is overwhelming, not in a touch or in a close manner, but in a relationship so deep that all fantasies are met without a physical touch; it is more than a closeness or whisper between lips to an occasional lover. The purest of love brings two such people together. The question is, why? Or how?

On that note, I'd like to respond. A divine connection or bond lives in your heart leads us to a person, that will guide us through these hard times in life. At times, those mountains and paths are so rugged and narrow, we can't possibly manage on our own. That spark comes alive, and the path is smoother, wider, and mountains so much smaller. Has this deep association taken the place of the Lord? Absolutely not, but heaven sent to smooth out the roads ahead and keep us strong and keep love in our hearts to manage anything that comes on our paths at any given time or place.

"Love at first sight with that person strikes to the heart and soul. It is meant only for us; we no longer blindly go through the days, long nights, or years by ourselves. A loving voice penetrates your thoughts and can make you swallow hard, thinking of years together and years to come. As night falls around you, the darkness may come, but you are never alone. A quick sound of their voice brings that spark back in an instant. We are the fortunate ones to find these partners to go through life. Never take it for granted or wish it away. You will forever be full of sadness that they are gone from your life. Stay at peace, love them in your heart and mind's eye and never let them go.

"God has a bigger vision for our friendships than we even can begin to understand."
—**Angela Suckett**

Thanksgiving for Essential Workers

Webster defines "essential" as necessary. As Thanksgiving Day is upon all of us, I sat and pondered over that term. I'm a mom of an essential worker, and I began to realize just how little that phrase means. In my eyes and many other friends and family I have spoken too, the word doesn't fit. Words are very important. They can bring tears, they can cut like a knife, or they can bring laughter. As the world continues to be in a state of flux, I stated to think about all the people this is affecting. We all have people in our lives, who can't see each other; quarantining has become our new buzz word for 2020, the faces of all of us covering smiles due to masks, but ultimately, it doesn't mean a thing.

As "frontline workers," your years of schooling never prepared you for such activities in the hospitals, ambulances, or firehouses. In our generation, never have you been asked to become a family member and soothe the hurting and wipe away the tears of loneliness. Compassion, a gentle touch and moments of kindness are your continued form of taking care of all these people. Not that these attributes didn't exist before; it is in your nature, but now there is a depth to the nurturing that has taken over for all workers. The touch of a hand, a sensitive shared tear, or a gentle chuckle can only be a bonus for anyone on death's door, alone and afraid of what it to come. As human beings we want to touch and give a gentle squeeze as a form of affection and have lost that power through this dreaded disease. Your strength is everlasting. You get the idea that the sounds of your voice may be the last one another hears as they go to be with the Lord, absent of family, friends, and beloved animals.

I again, sit and study the word *essential*. It just doesn't fit. You are all angels with long wingspans to carry the weight of the world on your shoulders right now. We all look to all of you for that compassion and strength we need to get through this. Being the most unselfish people on the earth, you always extend your hands and loving voices with covered smiles to help us make it through this crisis of humanity. We beg you all to continue in your tireless quest to make this better for each and every one of us, however we are affected. As angels, just your presence is all we need to get through. Thanks to all of you and know that you are appreciated, and we live for all your kind words. May God bless all of you and help you in your tired steps to go another mile, climb another mountain, and keep us safe. We love you all.

"Dare to reach out your hand into the darkness
to pull another hand into the light."
—**Anonymous**

IS THERE A FUTURE FOR OUR CHILDREN?

As I walked this glorious morning my mind was looking into my granddaughter's bright eyes of hope and a desire to know the future. What on earth can I tell her? How will I ever begin to explain to her what will be written in her textbooks. It is an impossible task. America the Beautiful seems to be choked up and being strangled by a force far beyond our hold. The strength of this monster is devastating our world, our families, and our human race. We are being put to the test day after day, hour after hour. The only way of coping is to look back to other times people have managed and survived such hardship. Can we compare those times of World Wars and the Depression era, with our current status of immigration problems and such vast unemployment and poverty?

How will be graded in the future? We tend to blame the previous generations, but we can't do that this time. I look back in an old Bible with my great-grandma's handwriting and see that families have gone astray. Looking at those names, I'm reminded of past stories the old timers tell the younger people that they all but ignore and find silly. It is in those stories that I have realized how far backwards we have gone.

Those were stories of the Depression era, when money was short, and times were hard. When things got tough, they did without and cut back on lifestyles. Stories of my mom, aunt, and grandparents living in a train box car for months, eating nothing but tomatoes from a close-by field was always just a conversation; now it has become reality for so many. The monster, the Covid-19 virus we face now, is just the topper. It is after many years of greed, overindulgence, and gluttony that our world has had to come to a big halt and look around with open eyes and see what we are headed for—a world that is foreign to us and nonexistent to the young at heart. We have just continued with our hate and ugly thoughts of other human beings, no matter who they are or what they believe in. Life has turned sour, and we are paying the price.

In our world today, we must take precautions and distance ourselves from one another. Such a crazy thought, but I'm enjoying the time people are taking to make sure each other are safe, along with kind words coming my way every day. I'm not too old that I don't remember a gentleman opening my car door for me, an older man tipping his hat to me with respect of one another. Those little courtesies that are long past and should have been remembered. Looking back to simpler times, I can see gentlemen removing their hats, and woman and children with their hands on their hearts as the American flag passed them by. Everyone knew the words to "America the Beautiful." Today one out of five in a public gathering would have to fake it. When we did something wrong, police didn't show up at your door. A neighbor would talk and work it out with the parents. We also would get our backsides tanned, and we didn't do it again.

Something that really scares me is that people aren't as honest as they used to be. Our government that we trusted with our lives is caught in lies and deceit without blinking an eye. Our society isn't as noble or as hard working as they used to be. Not all the current generation of people are the same. Many are hardworking and reliable, trying to make a place in this world for themselves. Unusual that co-workers' own families can't see their drive to achieve, and others are trying to teach them to turn their backs on hard work.

As we fight this new world in order to have a future, I send this book and the prayers in it to all mankind. Please study the past and learn from it.

I'm almost seventy years old. I have seen many things. I have raised a family, gave two infant sons back into God's arms, outlived my parents, and found a brother I never knew I had. Since I've been around awhile, I hope to hear those chimes of the bells that can be heard around the world as we fight to live another day. We must do it together, and we have to do it better. We are failing. We need to think about our little children of this world and seek a future for them. As we bring in the years ahead, let us use it as a new beginning and save ourselves and our world for the future of mankind.

Let's all work together to make a brighter future for these young people. Our medical expertise is valuable and will not let us down, but that is not all that will save us. A gentle nod, a bright smile, and the touch of a youngster's hand offers that light we are all missing. The years ahead are in our hands. We must be strong and make it work for these young, beautiful eyes, seeking a future from us. We can't let them down.

"When I approach a child, he inspires in me two sentiments—tenderness for what he is and respect for what he may become."
—**Louis Pasteur**

My Son

I believe. I believe we all have a purpose. As human beings we don't always know what that purpose is or where our strengths come from, we just have faith that our purpose is part of us to be valued and shared with others.

My dear son. You must believe. Believe in the answers that lay before you. You have the strength to survive any fallen hope. It lies within yourself dear one. The emptiness that you feel at times will disappear. You have great value and the ability to love greatly. I believe it is in your spirit and has been with you all these years. Don't let anyone tell you differently. There are many bright tomorrows to believe in and carry on in your heart. Hope is not gone. Be strong and find that truth inside of you.

There are answers that lie with you. I've taught you well, and it is all there for you to grasp and hold on tight, so it never slips away from you. You are strong and can survive anything God puts in your path. It is a long journey, a rough path. Our Lord didn't mean for it to be easy. You must work hard to throw away the emptiness and sadness. Put your fears behind you and fight to climb those mountains and struggles in your way.

You were meant to find a bright future. It is there for you for the asking. Sometimes tears come easily, but wash those tears away and take that deep breath and feel that sun God gave us on your cheeks. His hands surround you and circle you in the form of faith and hope. You have all of this within you. Find it and never let it go. I believe with the touch of a child, your child, you can feel God's opening that path for you. Those beautiful eyes guide us all to glory and see the innocence and purity that is meant for us to take in and guide us.

I believe you have lived through many storms, and by the strength of God's hands, you have come through and will continue to fight for what the Lord gave to you. Strength, passion, love, and sensitivity are all the ability you need right before you for a strong future. You must search hard and have faith that the Lord has surrounded you in His love.

So many years have gone by, so many struggles and temptations. I believe at one time you were ready to give in, give up, and head down that long dark hole, but something brought you back. I believe it was a little flicker that has remained inside of you all these years; it is that small light of hope for rescue. You've been rescued and ready to accept a brighter, stronger hold to make it out of the dark. You can do it. I have faith in you and so does our Lord. Neither one of us will ever leave you. You can depend on that. Feel our strength and passion for life. Share it with others and show you know the meaning of being loved here on earth and with your heavenly Father.

Climbing that tall mountain and fighting that long, rough stream brought you to this place. Safety, vision, loving care, and a direction lies before you. I am very proud of your courage and strength to right these wrongs and look to a brighter future. Open those wings and fly high as you can. Don't look down and be afraid; the peace will bring you forward into wonderful freedom. Knock off the chains of the past. The future is yours for the taking. This time is yours; you are almost there. With these healers around you, life will become a promise of beauty and light. Take this time to find yourself, grow, and get that smile back that I long to see.

At times you may feel far away from your family. Come to realize you are never alone, and we are all in your sweet dreams and beating heart. We are all very proud of you for facing the unknown. It won't be easy, and at times you may lose your faith, so fight harder and remember you are loved and thought of every day.

"To shine on those living in darkness and in the shadow of death, to guide our feet into the path of peace."
—Luke 1:79

My Daughter

A contagious smile, a gentle wave, and a kiss on the cheek are ways daughters communicate from the heart. So many years ago, the thought of being her mother came into my life. Who would have thought I would have been so honored to have her care placed with me? These daughters are from our heavenly Father and only in our presence for a very short amount of time. It is our job to nurture, to guide, and to give all the wisdom that we possess. Once into the world, daughters have their own lives and futures filled with dreams and hopes of lives of their own.

There are so many ways I want to say I love you. Let me forever take on the pain these rough roads can bring. I hope to always be a shining light in your eyes, a light filled with acceptance and tolerance as the years go by. In your young life, you have made me what I am today. Life for me never started until you came into my life. You are the love of my life. I can only assume that to others, that statement seems reserved for lovers. Not so. When the thought of you came into my life, all direction was made clear. Our connection as mother and child, and now as old and young women, we are friends and confidants—a bond that could never be broken.

Through these tired eyes, I see a woman with values and ideals far beyond her years. Inside you is where your heart beats on so many different levels. Your kindness, your compassion, and your ability to soothe the downtrodden are wonderful traits that I hope I had a hand in passing down to you. You see the world so clearly, it is quite remarkable. Always putting others ahead of yourself has given you power in your own abilities. That quality is desired by many. Never give that away. Compassion for others rest on your shoulders easily. Always remember that God gave you all these strengths and desires to treat His world with respect. Our bounty around us was created by the same God in heaven, who created you. He has given you so much awareness around yourself, including an ability to understand others' needs. At times, just listening rather than talking makes you so strong.

Listen to that voice in your head and never let it go silent. Our Lord speaks to you in His miraculous way. He knows your struggles and your sadness's. I'm here to keep you going and keep pushing forward. We complement one another, and even though you know my limitations, you are accepting of me, and for me, that is quite wonderful. God has a chosen few that He looks down upon and keeps the bar high. You will never disappoint Him. You were placed upon this earth to do good things, to spread a joy to align yourself with the sun, stars, and the moon, as well as all God's creations. You have made me very proud, and I hope we have many years to continue to find one another. That is in God's hands also.

My Daughter

As my daughter, you are not mine to show ownership. I'm simply watching over you for the Lord—watching you stumble from time to time, but always handing you that strength to get back up and whisper that you are ready to move on to the next adventure. As your mother, I only have you for a very short time. Always remember that I hold you in the highest regard; I'm am so pleased with that beautiful smile. Even with all the ups and downs of life, you make it look easy. God is happy to share these years ahead. My dear daughter, you came into my life in a quiet whisper, let me continue to show you the way. My dearest one, I'm so very honored to call you my daughter.

"Her ways are pleasant ways and all her paths are peace. She is a tree of life to those who embrace her, those who lay hold of her will be blessed."
—Proverbs 3:17

Dearest Baby

Today, you are just a smile behind your momma's eyes. A sweet thought, a dream waiting to come true. Your day will be one that will be always remembered throughout the years and one that will be thought about by many. We are so welcoming of you and hope you have many memories to share with us in the future as your life unfolds. As the years go by, you will have many ups and downs, and times of great sorrow and floods of sunshine coming your way because you are blessed with family and friends and more and more acquaintances than you can ever imagine.

Remember how much you are loved and welcomed into this world. Remember your momma will always be there for you, and as you grow from being mother and child, you will at some point become valued friends. Look back on the old photos of your lifetime and recollect the good and bad times with honor. Your momma and grandma will fill you in on the stories of your family and the life you may have forgotten. Your grandma is quite a character and will forever be your champion; come to her for peace in your life and long-lost memories, which only she can tell. Cherish those kitchen smells that will forever remind you of her. Look deep into her eyes for wisdom as you grow into a beautiful young woman. Even now, she is very proud of you.

The future is yours and worth holding in your small little hands. They will grow as you will offer the future of this world your independence, your knowledge, your honesty, and most of all your love of family, friends, and yourself. You are a beautiful young woman waiting to open your wings.

Enjoy your life and know we are all looking to you for a world of sweetness and beauty.

A Mother's Eyes

The earth rotates with all the awe that God intended. As children of the Lord, we have come to wonder and respect the land we are committed to. Life, as we have come to know it, is very fragile and can at times bring us to our knees in questions of our existence. The planted seed that finds the nourishment to grow and flourish is the basis of our souls. It can grow bright and full of excitement about the steps in our path. It can also be tarnished and spoiled with lack of love and nurturing.

When I look into my mother's eyes, I am overcome with her years of knowledge, overwhelming sincerity, and faith that our Lord has helped her to understand and use in her lifetime. Through these years, the path my mother laid before me has been full of challenge, a struggle at times, but never without her compassion and honor to help build me a better life for myself. The sun rises and sets every day on all God's people. It is up to us to take those rays and make them come alive in our days here on earth. We are never promised one day in this lifetime. Our readings tell us that it is up to us, people of the earth, to understand the needs for establishing this commitment to the world.

As I have matured, I have begun to realize the many paths and journeys we must all take and learn to develop our own lives as the world continues to ride throughout this universe. As time would have it, I have become aware of the beauty surrounding me in God's hands. After being told that a cancer had invaded my body, I felt a personal loss of not seeing my children grow old, living out my mom's years with her and directing her, and experiencing personal peace and warmth that a home can bring.

It was at this time, I realized, life had not been given to me as a promise, an expectation, or a right. It was up to me, with all the guidance my mother had given me through the years to be a fighter, a master of my own will, and spread that hope and belief she had trusted upon me over the years through my body. It was then I knew my mother had given me an incredible gift, one of faith, hope and determination to fulfil dreams set here on earth.

Through my mother's eyes, I see a brightness and a peace, one I will never let go of, throw away, or take lightly. It is from her compassion and trust in the Lord that our lives would be forever connected and that I have learned how to fight this disease. I remember through her that I have been given a valuable gift, the gift of the Lord in all His mercy. I will forever be strong and see my children grow old and give them these gifts of life, honesty, and survival in a tough, but wonderful world.

A mother can guide, she can persuade and try and turn those wheels for lifetimes of smiles, but as wonderful as those gifts are, we are human beings of age, and we shall remember that our smiles, our futures, and livelihoods are now our own. From our mothers, we have been given the paths to take and must tame them ourselves. We must remember those soft eyes at birth, the tug of a small hand, and the sweetness of a smile glowing within you will forever shelter the compassion and strength that a mother can bring. Let us never forget that image in our minds. It is forever lasting and one that will continue for generations to come.

A Mother's Eyes

"A mother dreams when her children are small, of all they will be when they grow tall."
—Jewish Prayer

My Brother

My dear brother, you have a strength within you that has always been led by our Lord. He has given you a spirit that I adore. A compassion for our God has always guided you in his direction, and in return, you have been given the trust and faith to speak His words and love for us as His children. I see the truth and feel your presence on many days we are apart. You are working for the Lord, serving him in every way you can, and I have been given the strength of giving and caring for others. You have given me this passion for life.

I'm not afraid anymore. You and my God have given me all the answers I need for this lifetime. I see it in your eyes and in our hearts as brother and sister. I see the truth every day of my life. You never need to feel alone when you are struggling. We are connected through life, and I will always be there. Together we have the strength to carry on. When life lets us down, we must look to ourselves for that inner glow that only Christ can place within us. You are my hero. Maybe you didn't know that. Life has so many twists and turns. We often feel like all the hopes are gone. That deepness and strength that only our God can give us are still there, my brother, and lie within ourselves.. We must hold on tight and look to each other no matter how far apart we are and take pride in the fact that we are never without each other and never alone.

It is a long winding road, and we are not meant to know where it leads. God wants it that way so that we have the faith and spirit within ourselves to continue with that strength. We can survive anything together, no matter how apart we are. It lies within us. We have a history, a connection, a bond, that will forever be true. Hold on tight and never let that go. I won't, and I know you have that power to carry on and know I'm always by your side. Hope is never gone, my brother, my friend. Always know I'm here through any occasion, through any fear you may have, and I know you are there for me too. Our power together is unlimited and will carry us through any storm.

"I guide you in the way of wisdom and lead you along straight paths. When you walk, your steps will not be hampered; when you run, you will not stumble."
—**Proverbs 4:11–12**

On that long trail, that tall mountain, you come back into my life and spread your wisdom and your joy into my being. I dream of it often and look forward to those days. We never know what is on the other side of that mountain. We must take chances and not break but have everlasting strength to keep going. I can keep pushing with you at my back. We can do this together. My love for you is overwhelming. I appreciate every moment we share, and it lies deep with me and keeps me going every single day. Those journeys are always going to be there. We must pull it together and continue to drive our strength in our Lord together. For that, I am so thankful to call you my brother.

"It's Finished"

So many good times, so many good days, with clouds bright and welcoming: those beginning days and months were like that. As with any parent, we hold so much hope and promise for the young child in our arms. With God's inspiration, this little life we hold so dearly is all so fragile, more than we would think possible. As the years go by, we all but forget that life is a mixture of good and bad. We all have hoped these issues would fade and not define us as people of God. For the strong, it is all the hope to overcome and know these dramatic traumas are in our minds and forgiven in our hearts. As children, we look to our mothers for an ongoing smile, a bright light in her eyes and those cheering words of wisdom we all live for, no matter what age we are in this life.

As your mother, I was always full of hope and forever willing to believe the best for my son. At times in your life, I came to find that was not always the case. I suppose at times we all live in a dull existence, a time when we know change should take place, but not knowing how to deal with the change. I found myself in such a place. Once I came from the fog and turned my eyes to our Lord, I began to see that change was needed to protect myself and my children. It was at that time, I began to realize and say to myself, "It's Finished." I was coming out of the darkness and into the light, the light of our God. I saw that brightness that can be lived every day with His help.

It is time for you, my son, to come out of the darkness and demand that "It's Finished." Break away from those chains and get excited about a future that is all yours. God meant for it to be this way. You are blessed and can learn from the past. A past of broken dreams and dark realities is over. Come to terms with this and live a life that you have earned.

We all must have vision for life. Knowing where you start is not important; it is where you end that is of value. Life is a mixture of sadness, success, failure, comfort, and pain. Encouragement and frustration, love and hatred, relief and sorrow cause you to struggle and consider giving up. Life is not perfect, but it is beautiful and needs to be cherished. We all take steps in a unique way. It is in God's hands, and with His guidance, you take those steps of courage with His hands on your shoulders.

Surround yourself in faith, the faith in Christ. You are a product of our God. He loves you and has shown you the way out of the darkness and will continue as you learn to fight hard and stay connected with his strength. His guidance will forever encourage you and keep you strong in faith. These storms were violent for you as a child, along with bumpy roads for the hardest journey possible. These storms have quieted and breaking forth is a brightness that may overcome you. Don't let it. It is a path for you and one to be curious about. The Lord has brought you to the light, and after years of fighting and breaking clean, He won't desert you and neither will I.

"I can do all things through Christ who strengthens me."
—Philippians 4:13

"It's Finished"

I am forever your champion and will hold fast to you in this lifetime. Remember you are loved and cherished, and I will forever have faith in you on your journey. We all must face those challenges; you know mine, but this passage is for you, my son. From the very beginning of your life, I knew you would be challenged because God expects us to dare, to cause conflict, and then to solve with His presence. You are on that pathway now, and it will end for you all to the positive. The Lord has already shown His presence in your life. The strength to overcome, the zeal to make it out of a total darkness, and the presence of mind to find work hard for all the good life has to offer, precious daughter, you look to for strength, and comfort is now in your life. With God's help and guidance, you will help mold this beautiful child into a young woman with all the passions that life has to offer her.

You are loved by many. Know the God's love is all encompassing, and He invites all of us to a future of wonder.

"Then you will go on your way in safety, and your foot will not stumble. When you lie down you will not be afraid; when you lie down, your sleep will be sweet."
—**Proverbs 3:23**

Our Lord's Work

The bright skies and wonderful sun are God's way of touching our cheeks as we fight through a world of confusion. The news reports bring sorrow and pain to each and every one of us. The dangers which face so many every single day of their lives are unnerving. Somehow, we manage to put one foot in front of the other, and we are guided down that long path. Sometimes dark and unyielding, we walk, run, or crawl toward a light that we can't look away from. We must all have strength to carry on with a smile that will only be inviting to the heartache of others.

A divine connection has brought us to this safe and cheerful little place. No anger, torment, or sadness exists here. It can't. Our Lord's work is carried on in these walls by people that have been chosen to lighten the load of others who choose to enter. In such a troubling world, I'm honored to be accepted with new friends with such an honorable cause. The cause is fighting for our God and sharing our inner spirits, an overwhelming power to face every day with a light chuckle, or glorious smile. Your strength carries on no matter how tired you are, and you give others hope. Helping at this shop is a part of you and your being. God has nurtured you for that reason. You never give up and never run away from giving of yourself and your time to others. People you see throughout the week look forward to your ongoing smile, your strong arms, and soft eyes. You may be the only person they see in a day, and leaving part of yourself with them is a gracious gift.

May God give us the strength and wisdom to continue helping others in need. Never forget you are much appreciated, even though it may be unspoken. You leave your mark every day. This treasure will never be forgotten.

"The Lord gives strength to his people;
the Lord blesses his people with peace."
—**Psalm 29:11**

A Runner's Story

A clear, sweet wind hits your cheeks like the brush of a child's kiss. Blowing through your hair and on your neck, the pureness goes through us all. Pinpointing that feeling is an art and one a runner feels every time one puts on those running shoes. The paths are long but never narrow. Others flying pass you with a kind thumbs up and a cheery greeting keeps us going, allowing your body to put one foot in front of the other without a stumble.

What keeps us going? What pushes us to continue no matter what the weather or the day's stresses? One simple answer lies in all of us. That passion, that inner voice of the Lord, hugs us with everything He's got, soothing our bodies to search for more strength to make it to that end goal. The whisper of His voice is our reason for living, and running every day, we can get out there. We all long to be in His grasp and feel that high at the end of the journey.

Life can be fearful, and sadness can take over at times. Those journeys and mountains to climb can be long, and at times too high to travel alone. As we pray for strength and direction, our paths can be curious to us. Our storms can rattle us in the simplest of ways, but we are taught from a young age to stand by Him for that added help and guidance. We do the best we can, and somehow, we are directed and stay strong in our Lord's bright light. We won't lose the battle and will continue to fight with everything we have.

I believe strongly in divine connections. As runners we have come together and met by chance, but not His. We have been directed to help one another, to give each other strength and the hope of healing for our bodies in our God's eyes. As the sun strokes our faces, we know this is the Lord's hand on us, guiding us to fight harder, and use all the strength He has given us to find our way. After a first run in the snow with white-covered trees and the cold hitting my face, I was immediately focused on God's bounty on this earth. We need to treasure everything around us and not take it for granted. With these surroundings, we can make it. All brings us the ability to drive forward. My life has forever been changed and these divine connections will also be with me forever. I appreciate all the love, big smiles, and hugs that have helped me move in the right direction to strive for more distance to see this earth in every way, every day. My best to all runners and friends considering such an adventure. Dare to walk or run on the high side. My plea to you, is do it for yourself, your body, and your love of God.

"Trust in the Lord with all your heart and lean not on your own understanding; in all your ways acknowledge him and he will make your paths straight."
— **Proverbs 3:5–6**

Joey's Christmas At Sea

Joe M. Leavey and Vivian Ann Leavey
Originally written 1962

*S*tepping aboard the old tub, I immediately was tuned into the vastness of the floating vessel. I have always dreamed of a naval career, but I felt it could never happen. But here I am, with dress blues, white sailors cap on my head, and spit-shined shoes keeping my feet warm and dry.

Leaving home certainly wasn't easy for me and my family. None of us had left our farm before, and the thought of eventually leaving the country was unheard of. Joining the Navy was an easy choice for me and a tough one for Mom and Dad. Not only was it hard for them to let me go, but it was also a matter of economics. We run the farm ourselves, so I will truly be missed. Now my brother Ben will have to fill my old boots. I'm sure he isn't thrilled about that, but they will manage.

Changing into the uniform of the day, I felt physically ready to take on my shift, but my thoughts were definitely elsewhere. Coming up from below to take my shift, I noticed the dark blue sky kept rolling above my head, looking more threatening and bleaker. The wind circled around me. This is my first time away from home and my first time away at sea. I love the Navy. I have made some good friends, and I have enjoyed my training on this old PT boat. The rough waters bounced me back and forth throwing my thin body to and fro. "I guess it's a sure bet we won't be seeing that Christmas star tonight." Joey was talking to himself, watching the water splash against the sides of the boat.

My relief will be coming up in about an hour. I sure will be looking forward to seeing him. I'm cold and feeling alone out here in this huge body of water. Suddenly a spray of salt water struck me in the face to make sure I was awake to complete my shift at watch.

Tonight, my thoughts are with my family and friends as they prepare for the Christmas festivities. They warm me through and through, especially tonight. All these feelings of love for others were the reason I made my decision to join up and serve this wonderful country.

Christmas Eve at my house has always been a special time. Not just because of the celebration itself, but the camaraderie, the closeness we all feel toward one another is a luscious time. My brother Ben and I forget about all the little indiscretions the year has brought about and become united. All the old feuds with neighbors are something of the past, and we just enjoy what we have. Wonderful isn't it how one night can do all of that? Tonight, is potluck because Mom will be preparing a huge turkey and all the extras. I sure will miss my favorite mincemeat pie. My mouth is watering thinking about all the terrific smells filling the house.

This year is even more special. We inherited Rosey, a mare that was no longer ridable due to an injury. So, we took her over as a broodmare. She is a gorgeous young lady, a chestnut with four white socks and a white star on her forehead. Rosey has a gentle personalit, but just enough spunk to make her special and smart too. She would grab a carrot out of my coat pocket every morning. I left Ben with that pleasure when I left to go overseas. Now she is ready to give birth anytime now. A first in our family, we have never had horses before. Some pigs and chickens were the extent of our livestock. We all have come to love Rosey and look forward to loving her little ones. It seems only natural that the event should take place this time of year.

Looking up to the clouds, I am disappointed to think I won't be able to see that guiding star. It has been a tradition to bundle up and go outside to view the star at midnight. It seems to be getting colder as I turn up the collar of my pea coat supplying extra warmth for me.

I can picture my mom and dad preparing all the food and trimming the tree with family and friends. They will be turning on the tree lights at midnight and having the traditional eggnog and Christmas toast. Only about fifteen more minutes.

My relief is finally here, bringing me a steaming hot cup of coffee. Handing me a paper from down below, Tom explained a message that had come across the wire for me. Looking at it, I couldn't help but smile and feel more warmth than I have felt in a long time.

Joey, you are a new uncle, Rosey had her foal at 11:58 p.m. Baby and mom are fine. Merry Christmas, son, we love you.

As I looked up at the sky, the clouds were blowing and moving around making way for the bright Christmas star. Joey turned, "There it is, Tom. That's what life is all about—to show us and guide us."

We both lifted our coffee cups for a toast. "Merry Christmas, Mom, Dad, and Ben, and here's a toast to you, Rosey and baby."

Afterthoughts upon Completion of My Book

If I have given the reader one second of peace, one moment of calm and knowledge that you are not alone in your life, I have fulfilled my purpose with this collection. My first love has been writing and sharing my thoughts on paper since I was a young girl, first in journal writing and then through children's books. At the age of twelve, my dad and I would sit after school, working on a story together, listening to music. Those were wonderful times, making beautiful memories, and preparing me for the roads of life ahead. That essay, "Joey's Christmas at Sea," very special to me, is included in these writings. I will conclude that effort was my first challenge at writing for others. I will leave my readers with these words to be remembered and consumed in your life time. I live by them as well:

> Life is what you make of it. Your choices are your own, and you have to live by them. Use all the resources you are given in your long path. Whether that be your ancestry, your education, or your experiences, with God first in your heart and soul, no harm can come to you. Keep the Lord first in

your life, live by example, and face every high mountaintop with His hands on your shoulders.

"Now may the Lord of Peace himself give you peace at all times and in every way. The Lord be with all of you."
—2 Thessalonians 3:16

Special Thanks

I can only give of myself and with these words in my collection, I have tried to accomplish this with many thanks to all of my family and friends for their guidance and patience in my hours of trying to get my thoughts down on paper. As some of these pages have cut deep into my soul, I'm thankful for the many that have given me a smile, dried my tears, and given me open arms of strength and wisdom.

God bless all of you, and may all the wisdom and strength you gave to me come back to you twofold.

With much love.

Vivian

About the Author

As written in the passages you just completed, you may want to know more about me as an author in today's world. Writing my thoughts has always been a pleasure for me, but often life gets in the way, such as having employment and careers to carry on through life. After college I began working at an area hospital, stating it was simply a place to hang my hat and I'd be there shortly! However, after eighteen years as a respiratory therapy professional, with small children at my side, I left the medical field and started working as a Montessori directress for the preschool set. After wonderful years of looking through children's eyes and guiding them to places unknown for seven years, I left my career there to develop more literary skills.

As an author of three children's books: *The Mysterious Neighbor*, *Taylor*, and *The Glass Teepee*, I was heavily involved with participating in Young Author weeks at elementary schools throughout Indiana, Southwest Michigan, and Ohio. Those were fun days of classrooms, young writers, hopefully encouraging youngsters to spread their wings and write about their lives.

Continuing to be directed by youngsters, I went back to my roots of teaching and got my teaching license. Teaching Family and Consumer Science at an area high school was both fulfilling and touched me deeply. Observing young minds develop and reach for the stars was a dream come true for me. After eighteen years of service, I retired and have since continued writing and filling my time with volunteer work for the Lord.

With the help of a student and his online skills, I was able to find the family I'd lost fifty-three years ago, not by tragedy, just life, and how it takes us through strange twists and turns year after year. We have reconnected, and I travel to see them when at all possible to understand our ancestry, get to know our family tree, and just have fun sitting outside around the fire, telling all the stories of all our pasts.

Life has its ups and downs for sure, but I have found through prayer, the love of family and a continued interest to achieve—anything you desire can be done. I like to live by these words:

"To be kind is more important that to be right many times. What people need is not a brilliant mind that speaks, but a special heart that listens."
—A Jewish quote

CPSIA information can be obtained
at www.ICGtesting.com
Printed in the USA
BVHW061811281021
619988BV00001B/1